VANCOUVER ISLAND
AND THE
GULF ISLANDS

VANCOUVER ISLAND
AND THE GULF ISLANDS

Photographs by
MENNO FIEGUTH

Introduction by
JACK HODGINS

Toronto
OXFORD UNIVERSITY PRESS
1981

To the Epp family, Tracy, Lorne, Gwyn, and Arnold,
who gave me a home on Vancouver Island.

MF

Title page plate: Dogtooth violet, Sayward

Designed by FORTUNATO AGLIALORO

© Oxford University Press (Canadian Branch) 1981
ISBN 0-19-540329-0

1 2 3 4—4 3 2 1

Printed in Hong Kong by
EVERBEST PRINTING COMPANY LIMITED

Introduction
by Jack Hodgins

The landscape still favoured by most photographers of these islands is the landscape of lush rain-forest jungle and violent coastline that seems to exclude—or at best ignore—humans: explosions of sea spray on rocky beaches; rotting half-buried logs giving birth to ferns and mossy trees and exotic parasite plants; lonely lakes where eagles perch on high skeletal snags; twisted arbutus trees clinging to coastal rock; intimidating snow peaks and delicate alpine meadows and spectacular waterfalls. All of these are here, all are here in abundance. Gravel logging roads will lead you deep into mountain valleys, up terrifying switch-backs to plateaus and glaciers and breathtaking views of fiord-like inlets. In these remotest areas, where the only sign that man inhabits this world is the occasional logging camp or tiny fishing village or the odd float house of some independent soul, wildlife still behaves much as if it had all this to itself. The wolf population of northern Vancouver Island is increasing its numbers at an impressive rate. Black bears root around in the town dumps with the same casual authority with which they scoop salmon out of streams. More than a thousand trumpeter swans, once nearly extinct, spend their winters on our lakes and river mouths and inlets. A confused or angered or hungry cougar has been known to attack a human occasionally. But when one of these graceful cats recently chased a dog right into its owner's kitchen, the intruder was just as surprised and alarmed to find itself there as the housewife who opened the door. The photographer in pursuit of only the wilder side of life on these islands might be as surprised and dismayed as that cougar to learn that people live here too.

Menno Fieguth is not one of them. His eye, which seems to seek out life in all its forms for celebration, has found plenty of evidence that these islands are home to people as well as to trees and wild animals. Even in the thickest corners of wilderness there are signs that people have been coming here for a long time, and for special reasons. Small settlements and peculiar ruins encourage us to see the history of these islands as the history of utopian colonies, most of which have failed to realize their original dream. From all over the world people have come, often in small groups, and once here have proceeded to make even smaller islands for themselves by creating exclusive societies dedicated to the pursuit of idealistic visions. At the far northern tip of Vancouver Island, for instance, a few abandoned buildings still sag on rocky headlands and in growing rain-forest where a group of Danes, in the early years of this century, attempted to create a farming community in a landscape so remote and hostile that now it seems they were doomed to failure from the first. A little to the south, on Malcolm Island, a community of Finns still lives in the tidy rows of wooden houses where their fathers and grandfathers created a socialist colony under the leadership of Matti Kurikka—despite the fact that the original goal of economic self-sufficiency had to be abandoned. At Hilliers, a weather-blackened picket fence surrounds an area where once a perfect replica of a Russian village stood, home to a community of Doukhobors led by a prophet who called himself Michael the Archangel. And a few buildings still stand near Nanaimo, too—setting for the scandalous history of the colony of Brother Twelve, another 'prophet', who gathered wealthy people from all over the globe with the story that the world was about to end everywhere except on Vancouver Island. Once these people had handed their fortunes over to him and moved onto his piece of land, he turned them into his slaves. Ironically a group of former slaves from the American South, who'd travelled across the continent by covered wagon and stage coach in search of true freedom, had settled on Salt Spring Island, not many miles away.

And then, of course, there is Victoria. It is not quite so easy to see this diverse and busy city as a utopian colony. Yet for those British officers who found England a disappointment after a lifetime of romanticizing the old country in the heat and isolation of India, this was a climate and a location where it was possible to manufacture an England that corresponded more closely to their nostalgic dreams. The city is of course a great deal more than the imitation England it once was (and that is advertised in tourist brochures), but a few shreds of that romantic vision still linger—in the dainty gardens that contrast so dramatically with the surrounding wilds, in the restored early architecture and the few cobbled streets, in the distinct accent preserved and perpetuated by several private schools in the area, and in the ritual tea at the Empress Hotel overlooking the harbour. Separated from the mainland by water and from 'up-island' communities by a mountain, Victoria continues to grow in its own unique and attractive way: a cultural centre, a government town, a university community, and a tourist attraction.

Today place-names reflect the origins of various searchers after the good life. Communities with Spanish names like Galiano and Finnish names like Sointula and Irish names like Kildonan are scattered amongst places with names contributed by local Indian bands (Cowichan, Nanaimo), as well as places with more British-sounding names like Courtenay, Sidney, and Cobble Hill. The strait that separates the islands from the mainland was named *Gran Canal de Nuestra Señora del Rosario del Marinera* before Captain George Vancouver renamed it in honour of his king (and only incidentally after himself).

People still come here from all over the world, some to retire in a friendly climate, others to begin careers in growing towns, still others to carve back-to-the-land communes out of the bush. But the utopia today's newcomers seek tends to be a little more materialistic than their predecessors' dreams. Used-car lots, fast-food outlets, and giant shopping malls are multiplying at an alarming rate along the highways. So are tourist attractions—some as natural as the protected trees in the ancient forest of Cathedral Grove, some as strange and deliberate as a castle made of glass, and some as alien and exotic as the replica of Anne Hathaway's cottage outside Victoria. The busiest dream-merchants may be the real-estate developers, who seem determined (to the eye of the nature-lover at least) to turn the islands into coast-to-coast subdivisions, all neatly packaged and serviced and bulldozed clean of trees. Turn a corner in even the remotest parts of the wilderness and you could be greeted by a developer's sign offering this piece of the world, this spectacular view, this wild utopia for sale at a certain price.

Despite evidence to the contrary, the population of these islands is not totally dedicated to exploitation and growth. Indeed, on the smaller islands the impression is precisely the opposite: a strong dedication to preserving things more or less as they are. Everywhere, and at all times, the population of all these islands will jump at every opportunity to celebrate something: nature, history, immigrant cultures, local skills, the arts, foreign holidays, the future. Fall fairs display the products of the rural harvest, Renaissance Faires sell the workmanship of potters and carvers and leatherworkers, Loggers Sports Days demonstrate the competing skills of men and women who work in our largest industry, an annual music camp shows off the artistic talents of young musicians from all over the country, Victoria Day parades and Canada Day parades celebrate our connections with the rest of the country and with the rest of the Commonwealth. No one has yet determined precisely what is being celebrated in the annual bathtub race across the strait to Vancouver, but whatever it is, this colourful event has become the most famous of them all, with competitors travelling from as far away as Australia to take part. All of these and more are excuses for community festivals, a public sharing of the pleasure there is in living here.

A woman who'd lived all her life in Saskatchewan said recently that, much as she loved to visit the coast, she couldn't possibly imagine herself settling there. The very notion seemed immoral to her. Life appeared to be far too easy. How could she enjoy any of this beauty, this life, if she didn't have to pay the yearly price of a long and uncomfortable and dangerous winter? Those who have been here for generations, as well as relative newcomers, have little time for such guilt. It's taken for granted here that man's surroundings should be as beautiful and benign as they are dramatic and awe-inspiring. The struggle ahead—amidst plans for bridges and tunnels and faster ferries to the mainland, amidst rapidly growing towns and the ugly spread of paved and plastic culture along the highways—will be to try to keep that wonderful sense of balance between people and wilderness that has been the unique and dominant characteristic of life on these islands.

1   Active Pass, with Mayne Island and the Vancouver ferry, seen from Galiano

2 Empress Hotel (1905), Victoria
3 British Columbia Parliament Buildings (1898), Victoria

4   Helmcken House, Victoria, built in 1852 by Dr J.S. Helmcken,
a leading citizen of early Victoria.
5   Craigdarroch Castle, Victoria. Built by Robert Dunsmuir in 1889,
it now houses the Victoria Conservatory of Music.

6　Butchart Gardens, Victoria
7　Crystal Garden, Victoria

8   Rogers' Chocolates, Government Street, Victoria

9   Beacon Hill Park, Victoria

10   Market Square, Victoria
11   Undersea Gardens, Victoria

12 Maritime Museum,
Douglas Street, Victoria
13 Canadian Imperial Bank of
Commerce (1858), Government and
Fort Streets, Victoria

14 Centennial Square, Victoria
15 Royal London Wax Museum, Victoria

16 'Anne Hathaway's Cottage',
Esquimalt
17 Bastion Square, Victoria

18 Wharf Street, Victoria
19 City Hall (1879), Victoria

20   Oak Bay, overlooking the Strait of Georgia
21   Malahat Drive, near Malahat Summit

22 View from Malahat Drive south towards the Olympic Mountains,
Washington, U.S.A.
23 Dominion Astrophysical Observatory, Victoria

24 St Michael and All Angels
Church (1883), Royal Oak
25 Holy Trinity Church (1885),
Patricia Bay

26 Cowichan Valley Forest Museum,
Duncan

27   Early Doukhobor house, Hilliers

28   Antique store, Hilliers

29   Randy Streit, Whippletree Junction, south of Duncan

30   Interior, the 'Butter Church' (1870), Cowichan Bay
31   Near Duncan

32   Painting the Ferry Terminal lanes,
Swartz Bay

33   Chief Officer Nic Collett, taking the B.C. ferry *Queen of Victoria* into Active Pass

34, 35   Vesuvius Bay, Salt Spring Island

36 Ferry docking at Otter Bay, North Pender Island
37 Saturna Island

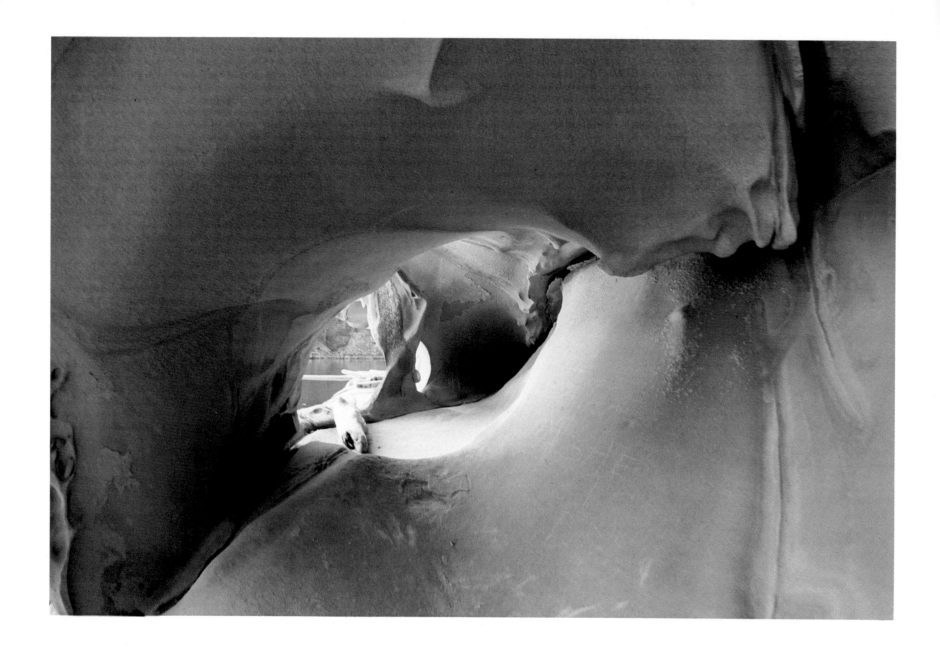

38 Rock Gallery, Retreat Cove, Galiano Island
39 Mt Baker, Washington, U.S.A., seen from Active Pass, Mayne Island

40 Derelict shipyard, Cowichan Bay
41 Cowichan Valley

42 Blockhouse, Hudson's Bay
Company Bastion (1853), Nanaimo
43 Marina, Nanaimo

44 Qualicum Beach and the Strait of Georgia
45 Port Alberni

46a   Near Buttle Lake, Strathcona Provincial Park
46b   Myra Falls, Strathcona Provincial Park
46c   Elk Falls Provincial Park
46d   Cascade, Little Qualicum Falls

47a *Amanita Muscaria*
47b Arbutus and daffodils
47c Skunk cabbage
47d Woodland fern

49   Cathedral Grove, Macmillan Provincial Park, Port Alberni

50 Tofino
51 Comber's Beach,
Pacific Rim National Park

52   Amphitrite Point Lighthouse, Ucluelet
53   Long Beach, Pacific Rim National Park

54   Alberni Inlet, from the *M.V. Lady Rose*
55   Wickaninish Centre Restaurant, Pacific Rim National Park

56   Evening along the dyke road between Comox and Courtenay
57   Seiners waiting for salmon fishing to begin, Green Cove, Alberni Inlet

58 Jousting on a log,
Salmon Festival, Campbell River
59 Renaissance Fair, Courtenay

60 Courtenay
61 Pa Jones and Misty, Courtenay

62   Dozer boats, Beaver Cove

63   Logging, Macmillan Bloedel, Kelsey Bay Division, White River area

64 Piglets on their way to a logging camp, Coal Harbour
65 Trucking lumber, White River

66   Evening, Hardy Bay
67   Aboard the Sointula ferry, Port McNeill

68 Longhouse, Alert Bay
69 Vancouver Island, seen from Alert Bay

70 Port Alice

71 Oyster fishery, Fanny Bay

72 Totem pole, Friendly Cove
73 Friendly Cove

74   *M.V. Lady Rose* leaving Bamfield for Port Alberni
75   San Juan Point, Port Renfrew

76 Barges, Sooke
77 St Mary the Virgin Church, the
'Easter Lily' Church (1879), Metchosin

78 Fisgard Lighthouse
79 Long Beach, Pacific Rim National Park

80 Dogwood, the B.C.
provincial emblem, Goldstream